You've Got This, Sister

Making the Mission Decision and Moving Forward

Kayla Rolfe Martin

Copyright © 2019 Kayla Rolfe Martin
All rights reserved.
ISBN-13: **9781712165539**

CONTENTS

Preface	5
Provo, UT	7
London, England	11
St. George, UT	18
The MTC	26
Cincinnati, Ohio	30
Rexburg, ID	51
Moving Forward	61

PREFACE

You will never fully know what to expect while serving a mission or what serving a mission is like until you live it. You've never experienced anything like a mission in your life—and that's okay. All you need to know right now is this: is serving a mission God's plan for me? With that knowledge, you can conquer any hurdle or concern that comes up in your preparation for and throughout your mission.

This book probably isn't going to answer a lot of the logistical questions you have about serving a mission. But before you close the book and put it back on the shelf, let me tell you this: God has *all* the answers you *need*. I can promise you that He's not going to give you all the answers you want, but if you read this book seeking the guidance of His spirit, I know He'll give your heart exactly what it needs. I know this because I have prayed for you, sister. Yes, you! I wish I could take you out to lunch, answer every single question you have, give you a big hug, look you in the eye, and tell you, "With God, you've got this," but for now this will have to do.

When I had the idea for this book (or, more accurately, when God placed the idea in my mind and told me I needed to make it happen) I talked to as many sisters as I could and asked them what their questions and concerns were about serving a mission. As I attempted to compile the answers to all of their questions, I realized I was writing a textbook. And that is not at all what God prompted me to write. A textbook is not going to speak to your soul. So, I'm skipping out on answering every question that's probably been racking your brain about P Days, transfer meetings, what to wear, and what exactly a zone conference is; and I'm going to share my story with you. Personal stories allow the Spirit to touch hearts—and that's what I want for you, sister. I want the Spirit to speak to you as you read. I want you to know that you are enough. When I stepped back and took a look at all the conversations I'd had, I realized that's really what every sister was seeking—an assurance that she is enough. That she has what it takes to wear the Lord's name on her chest for 18 months. So my invitation to you is to invite Him to be with you as you read about my experiences. Even though my mission story isn't exactly what yours will be, if you are seeking answers they will come as you read. And if we ever meet in person, I would be happy to answer every question about zone conferences, district meetings, and exchanges that you have.

PROVO, UT
October 2012

The morning of October 6th, 2012 started out like any other morning for me—hurrying around my apartment to get ready because I overslept yet again. I was supposed to meet my brother and his family who were in Salt Lake for the weekend and I was anxious to get out of my apartment and on the road. As I was scavenging the kitchen for something I could eat in the car, an eruption came from the living room where my roommates were watching general conference.

"Kayla, did you hear that?!" They exclaimed nearly in unison.

I hadn't, but my interest was definitely piqued and I decided I could postpone my trip to Salt Lake a couple minutes longer to find out what I had missed.

"They changed the missionary age! Elders can serve at 18 and sisters can serve at 19!" One of my roommates excitedly filled me in. I freaked out with them for a minute over the fact that we would all be eligible to serve within the next six months before finally heading out the door and getting on the road.

I made a valiant effort to pay attention to the rest of that session of conference as I listened to it on the radio during my drive, but I couldn't get that morning's news off my mind. I could honestly say that I had never given a thought to serving a mission.

At the time, being a 21-year-old felt like a lifetime away and, honestly, I figured I would probably be married by then. Now I was suddenly given the option to serve a mission two years sooner—which is basically a lifetime when you're a teenager—and could fill out mission papers within the next few months. My head swam.

I think it's important to rewind about 12 hours here, though.

On Friday night I checked my email for about the millionth time that day, knowing that I should be hearing back from the BYU International Studies program about my application to study abroad during the winter semester. When my inbox refreshed and I saw the fateful email appear I could hardly handle the butterflies that swarmed in my stomach. I hesitantly opened the email and then screamed out loud as I read the glorious words: "You have been accepted into our Winter 2013 London Study Abroad Program."

I would be leaving for a semester in London at just the time I would be able to submit mission papers. I had received a very strong and clear prompting that London was where I needed to be that winter so obviously a mission wasn't in the cards for me—or at least not for a while. Right? That's what I told myself over and over again during the next few weeks. But it certainly wasn't easy as my Facebook feed was filled with exclamations that nearly every girl my age (or at least that's what it felt like) was filling out mission papers and as my BYU classes each started with the reporting of multiple new mission calls every class period. I don't think I made it through a day throughout the rest of the semester without being asked by someone if I was going to serve a mission. I felt surrounded—and honestly a little suffocated—by the sudden pressure to serve a mission. I tried to pray about it, but my prayers were jaded by my fear of serving and of making the decision based on what was popular rather than what was really right for me. One thing I knew for certain was that I *did not* want to serve for the wrong reasons—only serving because that was the "status quo." If I was going to go, I was going to know that was God's plan *for me*.

By the time Christmas break rolled around and I headed home to spend the holiday with my family before taking off for London, I was mentally and emotionally exhausted and still as confused as ever about whether missionary service was in my future. I seriously needed some guidance and decided to meet with my bishop. We had a nice long talk—well, mostly he talked and I cried my eyes out. Luckily, he was inspired and told me exactly what I needed to hear. He read me scriptures, like D&C 6:22-24, which seriously sounded like they were written just for me and what I was feeling at the time.

My bishop was definitely inspired when he asked, "Can you think of a specific experience where you felt, one way or the other, that you did receive an answer?" In that moment, the Spirit brought an experience to my mind that I had completely disregarded when it happened. The Sunday before, I had been singing in the choir during sacrament meeting when I heard a voice clear as day tell me I would serve a mission. I was so busy thinking of doubts and concerns I disregarded the prompting almost as soon as I received it. Now, in this spiritual setting, I could not deny the answer God was giving me.

I was going to serve a full time mission.

I felt like a thousand pound weight had been lifted off my shoulders; the Bishop told me he saw a visible change. I finally received—and acknowledged—my answer and I could not deny it. I want to add here, though, that not everyone receives answers in the same way. The spirit speaks to us each uniquely. Just because you haven't heard a voice telling you to serve a mission doesn't mean that you haven't received your answer. God may tell you through your feelings and thoughts, through a dream, through an interaction with another person, or however else He sees fit. Just remember that all good things come from God. If you pray about it and feel good, move forward and see what happens. He won't lead you astray.

The next week was a whirlwind. Not only did my family celebrate Christmas, but I also prepared to leave for London and sped through my mission papers. Through divine intervention, I was able to complete all my interviews and medical appointments during the week of Christmas. That was nothing short of a miracle. I left for London less than a day after I submitted my mission paperwork to my bishop. What an emotional roller coaster.

<u>What I Learned in Provo</u>

- Pray with real intent
- It's none of your business what anyone else thinks of you
- **Spiritual questions deserve spiritual answers**

LONDON, ENGLAND
January- April 2013

I showed up to England emotionally drained and began to question my decision. The light that had illuminated my answer so clearly in the Bishop's office seemed to be growing dimmer with my stress. Those first few weeks in London were brutal. The adversary was working on me hard. I was overcome by homesickness that was physically, emotionally, and spiritually debilitating. I went to my classes in the morning and then rushed out into town on my own so I wouldn't have to talk to anyone. I was in such a bad place mentally that I knew I couldn't even get a sentence out without bursting into tears. I know that this might sound a bit crazy. I was living in London, a lifelong dream of mine. How hard could life really be, right? Trust me, that's exactly what I asked myself every day. However, realizing I "should" feel happy didn't change the awful, engulfing sadness that I felt.

Since then, I've learned that each of us has our own unique trials that are preparing us to become who God needs us to be and that none of us are doing any good by beating ourselves up because we have weaknesses. For me, that trial was loneliness. My parents and I have always had a really close, special relationship and I had only spent one semester (in Provo, three hours away from home) away from them. Now that I found myself in a foreign country surrounded by strangers, I was drowning in the loneliness that I felt. There were a couple weeks in particular that were painfully low. I spent my afternoons in McDonald's or Starbucks because those were the only places that I could access free WiFi to communicate with my parents. I begged for them to fly across the world and come rescue me or to buy me a plane ticket home. I vividly remember sitting in a McDonald's crying like I had never cried before while talking with my mom on the phone and having multiple strangers come up to me to offer tissues and ask if everything was okay. You know you're a mess when strangers are brave enough to offer you help. I was convinced that I couldn't serve a mission. If I couldn't handle one semester away from home how would I ever be able to handle 18 months away with only a weekly email as a means of communication?

Luckily, even though I know it was incredibly hard on them as well, my parents were inspired to encourage me to stay in London. At that point I didn't know where else to turn so I began to turn to God. Slowly, but surely, as I surrendered myself and my fears wholly to him, I started to break free from the chains of loneliness and sadness that were binding me. I remember one night in particular when I couldn't hold myself together because of the homesickness that was overcoming me. I rushed outside our flat and called my parents—even though I knew it would cost us an arm and a leg. I couldn't take the loneliness I was feeling for even a second longer. My loving parents felt impressed to share with me something they'd discussed in Sunday School that day. It was part of Joseph Smith's account of the first vision. He says,

"Immediately I was seized upon by some power which entirely overcame me, and had such an astonishing influence over me as to bind my tongue so that I could not speak. Thick darkness gathered around me, and it seemed to me for a time as if I were doomed to sudden destruction.

16 But, exerting all my powers to call upon God to deliver me out of the power of this enemy which had seized upon me, and at the very moment when I was ready to sink into despair and abandon myself to destruction—not to an imaginary ruin, but to the power of some actual being from the unseen world, who had such marvelous power as I had never before felt in any being—just at this moment of great alarm, I saw a pillar of light exactly over my head, above the brightness of the sun, which descended gradually until it fell upon me.

17 It no sooner appeared than I found myself delivered from the enemy which held me bound. " (JSH 1:15-17)

I felt the Spirit overcome me as they read the account to me. The Spirit witnessed to my heart, as it will to all our hearts, that the adversary had engulfed me in the same cloud of darkness. In that moment of clarity I realized that the adversary was doing all he could to keep me from serving a mission. He was literally binding me, as he had Joseph. It was now my responsibility to exert *all* of my power to call on God. It was time for me to take action. My dad then felt impressed to give me a blessing over the phone. I had no idea how badly I needed that. As he spoke through the Spirit, light started to filter into the darkness that had overcome my heart. When we hung up the phone that night I felt a little bit lighter. I was able to walk back into the London Centre without bursting into tears. I now knew what I needed to do. I needed to call on God.

After that experience I would stay up at night, in my bottom bunk bed with a little flashlight, reading the Book of Mormon and clinging to the precious comfort that it brought. As I committed myself to having daily spiritual experiences, the light of Christ once again filled my countenance. Although Satan valiantly tried, he could not take away or change the answer I received from God. I began to feel more like myself and to more fully experience and appreciate the peace and joy that can only come through the Atonement of Jesus Christ.

The adversary is real and he knows our potential—often better than we do. He will do anything in his power to stop us from accomplishing God's plan for us. However, as we rely on God, we will always be delivered. Even if it's in the very moment that we're ready to sink into despair. When looking back on this experience, my parents say that I wasn't myself during those dark weeks. Even from thousands of miles away they could tell that my usually bright countenance had grown darker. As I started to rely more on the Lord and really sought to access his Atonement, they saw His light once again enter my countenance. It was a powerful learning experience for all of us.

Over the next couple of months I made dear friends and enjoyed exploring England as I anxiously awaited my mission call. I would later come to realize that the time I spent in London was preparing me for my mission in ways I couldn't have imagined. Having to fight for my answer to serve and learning to rely solely on God to retain that answer helped me to love my answer. I truly believe that I would not have served my mission if I had not spent that time in London and gone through the experiences there that I did. I believe that God prompted me to spend that semester abroad so I would be prepared to serve him faithfully and wholeheartedly on my mission. He taught me that with Him I was strong enough. I was brave enough and bold enough. And with Him you are, too, sister. I have no doubt that He is directing the path of your life more intricately than you know.

A week before my call arrived, my study abroad group left for an adventure in Paris. As excited as I was to fulfill my lifelong dream of going to Paris, there was one catch—I knew my mission call would *(probably)* be arriving in London that week. Paris was definitely a good distraction from waiting for my call but let's be honest, I was more than ready to get back to London the Saturday our trip came to an end. The train ride from Paris to London was probably one of the longest experiences of my life. When we finally got to London I was a ball of nerves and literally ran like a crazy person through the train station, to the underground, through my tube connections and stops, to Palace Court, the street I lived on. It was actually probably quite the sight considering I was hauling all my luggage from Paris. Everyone in my group was just as excited as I was but I had lost all of them by this point thanks to my mad dash. I realized what a wreck I was and slowed my run to a brisk walk down Palace Court so I could attempt to collect myself and say a very heartfelt prayer. *The moment of truth.* I walked through the door with my gaze glued to the mail mantle and there it was: a white envelope with my name on it and the Church of Jesus Christ of Latter-day Saints stamped in the corner. I screamed, grabbed the nearest girl and hugged her so tight she probably couldn't breathe, and started bawling. I called my parents and cried with and hugged everyone as they got to the Centre. The time was set to open my call 30 minutes later. After setting up a Google Hangout with my whole family, gathering everyone in the parlor, and going through every possible emotion, **it was time**.

"Dear Sister Rolfe: You are hereby called to serve as a missionary of The Church of Jesus Christ of Latter Day Saints. You are assigned to labor in the **Ohio Cincinnati** Mission."

Screaming. Crying. Trying to figure out what language I'm speaking (English, thank goodness). Hugging. Crying. Pictures.

This is all pretty much a blur. All I remember is feeling the spirit so strongly and knowing this was the perfect mission for me.

When I calmed down enough to read my call packet, I discovered that Heavenly Father knew me even better than I realized. I would be serving in the small town, USA suburbs of Cincinnati-- my dream mission, believe it or not-- and the city my mom and I had traveled to the summer before and fallen in love with. I couldn't help but be filled with a sense of love and closeness to my Father in Heaven as I realized He had been preparing my path all along. As I looked back over the experiences I'd had since the age was lowered in the October general conference, I couldn't deny God's hand at every turn. I was able to receive my own answer very strongly and clearly, I was able to fulfill my dream of living in London, and through it all I was prepared to serve the Lord with all my heart, might, mind, and strength. The fight for my answer made the call that much sweeter. I'm so grateful for a Father in

Heaven who knows me perfectly and loves me enough to be involved in the details of my life.

What I learned in London

- God is directing your life. Trust in that.
- You are never truly alone.
- Don't be afraid to ask for help or for a priesthood blessing. If you're in a circumstance where you're not able to turn to family, there is always someone in the Church willing to listen and administer. All you have to do is ask.
- Let Christ in.

On the Thames River in front of the London Eye

My entire study abroad group and I just after I opened my mission call.

ST. GEORGE, UT

April-July 2013

I arrived home from London almost three months to the day from the time I would report to the MTC. I naively thought that I had conquered all my pre-mission trials in England. However, as the days and weeks drew closer to my departure I began to let doubt and fear creep in once again. When it all came down to it, leaving my family for 18 months to talk to strangers all day terrified me. I felt like I had no idea what to expect and that made me that much more apprehensive. I grew up in Utah, where the missionaries in our area covered our entire stake and the St. George Temple Visitors' Center—so I hardly saw them at church and only remembered having them over for dinner once or twice. I started to realize that I frankly had no idea what a missionary really did. I didn't personally know any sisters who had served so I began to research. I tried looking up sister missionary blogs but didn't have a lot of success with that. I found one book directed toward sisters but it was kind of a downer and honestly made me more nervous about what I was getting myself into (a big reason why I'm now writing this!). I felt unsure and unprepared. I remember lying in bed, unable to sleep, and wondering what I could do to get out of going. I couldn't figure out a really good reason to stay so I figured I might as well go. Really inspiring, right?

It wasn't just my own mind working against me, though. There were outside forces as well. Just to give you one example, I'll share with you a blog post I wrote on June 20, 2013—less than one month before I left on my mission.

"Everyone told me how hard the adversary would work on me before my mission, and trust me he has, but I never thought I would end up in the hospital! Last night I decided to go for a run after dinner. I was having a hard time breathing, but just chalked it up to being out of shape. By the end of the run my throat was burning so I decided it must be allergies. I hurried home to take an allergy pill. By this time my hands were also burning—not good. The back of my mouth started to feel numb and I got a little panicked. I decided to hop in the shower in case there was still pollen in my hair bugging me or something. After being in the shower for about 5 seconds I realized my throat was getting worse so I ran and got another allergy pill (something I NEVER do.. these pills are super strong and make me extremely drowsy, but it was that bad). My dad came in the kitchen and I asked if I was going to survive, totally teasing me for being a drama queen, but when I broke down in tears and tried to talk to him, but couldn't, he knew something was wrong, too. We got my mom and my dad called our home teacher who is a dermatologist while I headed back to the shower hoping washing my hair would still help. I barely got the shampoo on my head when I heard clear as day "you NEED to get to the hospital, NOW". I followed the prompting, shampoo still in my hair and soaking wet, threw on the nearest clothes, and got my parents. We sped to the hospital. Seriously, I've never seen my dad drive like that in my life. I could feel my throat swelling as we drove, it was getting hard for me to breathe, and I started to get really freaked out thinking that soon I wouldn't be able to breathe at all. Luckily when my dad dropped us off at the ER it was empty! A doctor got me in a wheelchair and rushed me back to a room. Another tender mercy, I saw a good family friend who is an ER doctor on the way and he immediately came to my rescue. They got an IV in me, pumped me full of drugs, hooked me up to all kinds of machines, and asked me a bunch of questions I couldn't answer. When the drugs started to kick in I got so woozy I thought I was going to pass out. My heart was also racing like crazy from the medicine—freaky. My Dad gave me a blessing and told me that everything was going to be alright and I felt calmness finally wash over me. The nurse laid me down and I was overcome by sleepiness. I had two super drowsy allergy pills in my system and now they were filling me up with Benadryl, after all. Every time I would start to drift, though, my body would start shaking like crazy. It got so bad that I couldn't take a breath without shaking all over. So they wrapped me up in a few nice warm blankets and I was out like a light. I honestly have no idea how long later, could have been a few minutes, could have been a few hours (I was seriously out cold), a nurse woke me up and told me I could go home! They unplugged me, wrote me a million prescriptions, and sent me on my way. Honestly, I was pretty freaked out to go home. At this point I could breathe but still couldn't talk very well and the doctor told me the swelling could reoccur, *how comforting.* I was terrified to go to sleep because I kept having the thought my throat would swell up while I was sleeping but I would be so out that I wouldn't realize and wake up. Luckily, I made it through the night!

The doctor told me it was definitely a food allergy, but I've never had an allergic reaction to food before and we have no idea what it was. Scary! This really freaks me out because I don't know what food to avoid and if this happens on my mission it could take me a lot longer to get to a hospital. Yikes.

However, I'm so grateful to my Heavenly Father for prompting me to go to the hospital when he did. I'm so grateful for my parents for responding so quickly and keeping me calm. Even though I was freaked out thinking of all the possibilities that could happen, I was comforted by my Father in Heaven the whole time and knew he was telling me that everything was going to work out. I'm grateful no cops were around when my Dad was driving 65 in a 25. I'm grateful my close friend was working in the ER. That was such a comfort to me. Even though last night was a little traumatic, it could have been so much worse. I feel so blessed to have my health and safety. I was definitely watched over last night."

I'm telling you, if something can go wrong before your mission there is a good chance it will. I'm not saying this to scare you, but to make you aware! As I shared in my blog post, God was with me and He is with you, too. He can help you get through any trials or roadblocks that may arise before you leave. This may be a difficult time. Your faith my waiver and that's okay. You're not alone. If you'll allow Him, God will carry you through the obstacles you may face before your mission. Rely on whatever faith you may have, even if it's only a mustard seed at times, and do your best to keep moving forward. No weapon that is formed against you shall prosper (D&C 71:9). Remember that often the greatest trials of your life will precede the greatest miracles and blessings. Hold tight and trust in good things to come.

After my hospital incident I had a follow up appointment with an allergy specialist. He tested me for all possible food allergens. The result: nothing. Everything came back negative. So, he tested me again, which is not a very pleasant experience, by the way. The second set of results showed: nothing. He was surprised and confused, but let me know that the best allergy specialists in the world were located in Cincinnati. He had no idea that's where I was called to serve at the time he gave me that information, but I knew that God was once again looking out for me. I put a major amount of faith in God from this point on. I had this recurring nightmare of going into anaphylactic shock again on my mission because I had no idea what to avoid since all my test results were negative, but reassured myself that God had placed me in the very city where renowned doctors would be waiting to rescue me. I started to wonder if that was the reason I was called to serve in Cincinnati. Thankfully, in case you're wondering, I never had any allergy issues on my mission or since! I think God was just testing my faith in Him and my willingness to serve with my whole heart.

After this experience I began to really throw myself into my preparation. I attended the temple more regularly, studied the Book of Mormon like I never had before, spent as much time with my family as I possibly could, and faithfully watched The District (which I thought was totally cheesy but kind of loved anyway). I felt my excitement begin to grow as I shifted my focus from fear to faith. It all came full circle when I was asked what scripture I wanted on my missionary plaque. My favorite scripture, which I hadn't thought about in a while, is D&C 6:36:

"Look unto me in every thought; **Doubt not, Fear not.**"

I had been doing the exact opposite of this! Elder Jeffrey R. Holland says "once there has been illumination, beware the temptation to retreat from a good thing. If it was right when you prayed about it and trusted it and lived for it, it is right now. Don't give up when the pressure mounts. Certainly don't give in to that being who is bent on the destruction of your happiness. Face your doubts. Master your fears." **Facing doubts and mastering fears can sound daunting, but with God it's possible to do both. Don't retreat from a good thing.**

While we're on the topic of mastering fears, one of the concerns that many sisters expressed to me was, simply put, the fear of missing out. Aside from missing out on family time and events, they were worried about missing out on opportunities in their own lives. What if I have to give up a scholarship? Or a dream job opportunity? Or a marriage proposal? These were concerns that I had as well. One of the opportunities I was afraid of missing out on was marriage. I was so young, but a year and a half feels like a really long time when you're 19! For about a month before I left on my mission I had myself convinced that I was supposed to marry someone I had been dating before I went to London. Looking back, I can see that my actions and emotions were completely based on fear. I was afraid of serving a mission and I was afraid of missing out on the opportunity to get married while I was serving. When I discovered that the boy I thought I should still be dating was actually now dating someone else I was able to move past this fear and move forward.

When dealing with your own fears, I would like to remind

you that this decision is between you and the Lord. Ultimately, He knows what path you need to take and what is best for you at this exact time in your life. If you feel like God is nudging you toward a mission I promise that He will consecrate those 18 months to make you a better student, employee, wife, mother, or whatever else you're aspiring to be, than you could ever become on your own. I'm going to talk more about this later, but please don't let the fear of missing out deter you if it's something that's holding you back. Face your doubts. Master your fears. God is with you.

If you're struggling with mastering your fears and wondering if God truly is with you I would invite you to attend the temple as often as you can. Temple attendance was one of the greatest blessings that helped me stay on the path toward my mission. In the temple I was reminded of who I am and what God's plan for me is. I felt the spirit there like nowhere else and was strengthened to be able to put my doubts and fears aside. You will also be blessed to receive your endowment before you leave on your mission. Prepare for that by taking advantage of the church's online resources and attending temple preparation classes. Some of the best advice that I received when I was preparing to go through the temple was to focus on the Spirit and not worry about remembering or understanding everything all at once. You have your whole life to do that! It's normal to feel a little nervous before going through the temple for the first time, but as you focus on what you're feeling while you're there, the spirit will be able to speak to your heart and you will find the comfort and guidance that you're seeking. Depending on where you serve, you may not have a temple available to you during your mission so I would encourage you to spend as much time there as you can before you leave. It will be a great source of strength to you in withstanding the trials that we've talked about. Our dear prophet, President Nelson, has said, "Our need to be in the temple on a regular basis has never been greater. I promise you that the Lord will bring the miracles He knows you need as you make sacrifices to serve and worship in His temples."

What I learned in St. George

- The hardest moments of your life occur right before the greatest blessings
- Don't retreat from a good thing
- Focus on the positive
- Never stop your steps to the temple

With my family after my mission farewell

THE MTC
July 2013

On July 9th I don't think I slept a wink all night. July 10th was the day that I began my journey as a missionary. I want to share this day with you directly from my journal:

"I woke up at 4:45 this morning and could not go back to sleep. At 6:30 I got up and tried to get ready but felt miserable like I had the flu. Dad gave me a father's blessing and I managed to get myself together enough to leave. I luckily slept most of the car ride and got feeling better enough to eat half a slice of Great Harvest bread when we got to town—great last meal, right? We headed to the temple to take pictures and things got pretty emotional. When we pulled up to drop me off I was a hot mess but my dad lovingly told me to suck it up and forget myself and go to work. We pulled up, I hugged my parents and Mandi [my sister] one last time, and my host missionary took me to check in. They gave me a name tag and just like that I was a missionary! This first day has been pretty incredible. I felt so sick I could hardly move and I was crying like a baby and then the second I stepped onto the MTC campus I was perfectly fine. Miracles are happening here already!"

I spent most of the drive from St. George to Provo thinking of ways to get out of going to the MTC that day. The physical sickness that had taken over my body was clouding my mind as well. I was definitely letting my doubts and fears take over the illumination I had experienced. When we were in the car driving the short distance from the temple to the MTC I kept telling my dad, "Don't turn yet!" every time he got to the light next to the MTC campus. But when I finally gave in to the Spirit, and to God, and took a huge step of faith onto that campus, the fog of doubt and fear was immediately lifted. It was like nothing I've ever experienced. Like I recorded in my journal, it was nothing short of a miracle. Sometimes all it takes to dispel the darkness around us is one step into the light, or in this case, onto the MTC grounds.

The rest of my entries from the MTC are like reading about a kid in a candy shop. Giddiness, pure joy, and contentment ooze from the pages of that journal, you guys. I didn't feel an ounce of homesickness, which you now know is a pretty big deal for me. Being at the MTC was a spiritual high that I will never forget and was a huge blessing to me after the nerves I had been facing for the last several weeks and months. I'm so grateful that I didn't give up when the pressure mounted, but that I was

able to face my doubts and master my fears with the help of my Savior.

<u>What I learned in the MTC</u>

- The more spiritual experiences you have, the happier you are
- Focus on others! When you're thinking of ways to serve your companions and those you teach, you won't have any room for homesickness.
- Getting a letter tops the feeling of receiving even the best Christmas present when you're a missionary

My MTC companions and I in front of the Provo Temple

Pointing to our missions on the infamous MTC World map

CINCINNATI, OHIO
July 2013- December 2014

Honestly, I could write a whole book just about my time serving in Cincinnati. But what I want to focus on here is how God took care of some of the biggest concerns I had about serving a mission. The three biggest concerns I had just so happened to be the overarching concerns that the sisters preparing for missions that I talked to had, so that's what I'll focus on here.

Family

First, how will I cope with homesickness and missing my family and the things going on in their lives? I have a very close-knit family so this was a big concern of mine. The experiences that I had in London helped to ease my mind a bit on this topic, but I was still nervous about being away from them for so long and only being able to communicate with them through email once a week. Just since I've been writing this book, that policy has changed. Hopefully being able to communicate more openly and frequently with your family will help to eliminate this concern for you, but, for added comfort, I'll share my experiences with you.

I want to start by sharing a thought that you've probably heard before if you've been a member of the Church for very long. Missionaries leave their families for 18 months so that others can be with their families forever. Now I want you to take a minute and really think about that and let it sink in because it's not just a cute saying for a plaque to give a missionary mom—it's 100% true. And that was something that really kept me going. I couldn't imagine having my family for anything less than eternity and I wanted everyone to know that was possible for them, too. You can literally change your family's story from "until death do we part" to "for time and all eternity." What greater blessing is there in this world than that?

However, even with this knowledge, I knew that it would be really hard to be apart from my family for a year and a half —just like it was in London for just a few months. As I described before, I've always been really big on family time. It's something that I crave. You can ask my husband now and he'll tell you that he and I and our kids would be by each other's side 24/7 if it was up to me. I honestly didn't know how I would live without my family during my mission. But God did.

A month or so before I left I started searching online for sister missionary blogs. You could probably find quite a few of those pretty easily now but at the time there weren't as many sisters serving, so I was only able to find a couple. I found a sister serving in Cincinnati (my mission!) so I started faithfully following her blog. She was serving in an area around the east side of the city and living with the sweetest family in their beautiful home. Through the stories and pictures that she shared on her blog, I was given so much comfort about going to Cincinnati. Despite the struggles that she shared, her mission seemed picture perfect to me. My mom followed her blog along with me and we both talked about how fun it would be for me to serve in that area and live with that cute family. However, I knew that my mission covered parts of three states and that my chances of ending up in that exact area were probably pretty slim.

Let's fast forward now a few months to July 25th, 2013. My first transfer meeting. I had been in the mission field all of 1 day. Transfer meetings are a lot of fun, but as a brand new missionary it was a bit overwhelming to be in a room of over one hundred missionaries who all seemed so much older and more experienced! Anyway, we all got seated and the assistants to the mission president started reading out who would be companions and what areas they would be serving in. The other new missionaries and I were anxiously awaiting our assignments. You could literally feel the excitement in the air. It felt like a lifetime waiting for my name to be called! Then, finally,

"In Eastgate, Sister Parker will be training Sister Rolfe."

I got up and headed to the front of the chapel where I was greeted by an adorable little redhead with the biggest and most comforting smile. We hugged, sat down together, and listened to the rest of the meeting. After the meeting ended, we loaded up our bags and headed toward our new area—Eastgate—with the member who had driven Sister Parker there. I asked as many questions as I could think of on the drive and was so anxious to get started as a real missionary! Before I knew it we were pulling up to a beautiful home. I figured this was the member's house who had driven us because missionaries live in apartments, right? Well, often yes, but in this case this was actually our home. I was shocked and so excited. It had a familiar feel to it and I figured that was just the comfort of the Spirit telling me I was in the right place. We headed inside and down the stairs to put our things in our rooms and that's when I saw it--- a picture of the sister whose blog I had been following before my mission. I was in shock. Out of all of the areas in my mission, I was actually starting my mission in the very home and with the very family that I had day dreamed about for all of that time! After that moment, I could not deny that God knows me very personally and that I was, in fact, exactly where I was supposed to be. I ended up serving in Eastgate twice on my mission (to my complete and utter happiness) and was there for just over half of my mission. The family I lived with there, the Blackhams, became my second family. As I've read back through my mission journals I can't count how many times I wrote that I felt like my companion and I and the Blackhams were a little family. To this day, I consider Brother and Sister Blackham (Mama B and Papa B) my family and don't know what I would do without them in my life.

While I was serving in Eastgate living with the Blackhams, I received a letter from my family telling me that my cousin had been called to serve in Cincinnati! I have a lot of cousins but I'm at the younger end of the family and don't have many around my age. This cousin, Sister Ryan, is the cousin closest in age to me. I was thrilled that she would be joining me in Ohio and hoped that we would get to see each other a few times. Well, once again, God had better plans in mind for us. Sister Ryan was also trained in Eastgate, but unfortunately I had already been transferred to another area. However, when I was transferred back there were two sets of sisters in the ward and we got to serve in the same area! We went on exchanges together and got to be companions for a couple of days. It was a huge blessing and a comfort to me to have a little piece of home and family right there with me. I remember one specific experience where our zone (about 20 missionaries serving in the areas around us) was able to go to the temple together. From an email I sent my family:

"I was one of the first sisters in the celestial room. As I sat there I felt so peaceful, but I also felt like something was missing. I realized that the last time I was at the temple was with most of our family and I missed that. It was so special being there as a family and now I miss and love you all more than ever so it was really tugging at my heart. Then Sister Ryan popped into my mind and I realized I was at the temple with family! I couldn't wait for her to come into the room so I could just give her a big hug. What a blessing. I'm pretty sure this was one of the reasons He let us serve together."

Sister Ryan and I ended up spending the last transfer of my mission as companions. We had a lot of fun telling everyone that we met that we were cousins, or kin as they would say in the Midwest, and I felt so close to home serving with her by my side. If missing your family is a concern of yours, let me tell you that God will take care of you. He will probably answer your prayers in different ways than He did mine, but I hope that my experiences have testified that God does know the concerns and desires of your heart and that He will answer your prayers in better ways than you can even begin to imagine. He will not leave you alone or comfortless, and your family will be blessed immensely because of your service. Elder Holland promises, "that because of your faithful response to the call to spread the gospel, He will bind up your broken hearts, dry your tears, and set you and your families free. That is my missionary promise to you and your missionary message to the world."

Companions

The second concern I want to talk about is companions. It can be a little daunting to think about spending all of your time with a complete stranger. I was definitely nervous about it! While I'm not going to lie and say that every one of my companions and I got along perfectly and loved every second of our time together, I will say that I love each and every one of my companions and that I cherish our relationships. I know that God placed each of them in my life for specific reasons and to teach me lessons that I could not have learned on my own or with anyone else. Yes, you will have days where you spend a few extra minutes in the bathroom just to get a little alone time, but overall, with the right attitude, you will come to love and appreciate each of your companions.

Something that was ingrained into the missionaries in our mission by our mission president's wife was the inspired saying, "find what's right." When you're with one person literally all the time it's really easy to start seeing and focusing on flaws or little things that bug you. But let me tell you, you are not going to have the Spirit with you if you do that and you are not going to be very happy. Your relationship with your companion will thrive when you focus on finding what's right with each situation that you're in—even, and especially, the frustrating ones. Learning to do this will bless your life not only during but after your mission, as well. Finding what's right can apply to really any relationship that you have, but one big and very important one will be with your spouse. Nothing will prepare you for marriage (or at least the living and spending all your time with one other person aspect) like serving a mission and having a companion! There was a famous quote that went around our mission about one of the elders telling our mission president's wife that he hoped his wife was just like his companion because they got along so well. While this may make you laugh, as it did us, learning to love and live with your companions will be the best marriage preparation you can find!

    I love all of my companions dearly and two of my companions, Sister Bowers and Sister Fox, are the best friends that I've ever had. I talk to both of them nearly every day and it's something that I always look forward to. They have each helped me get through some of my most difficult trials and I don't know what I would do without their friendship! They know me on a deeper, more meaningful level than any of the other friends that I've had. I actually struggled with having sincere, meaningful friendships when I was growing up and it was something that I always hoped for. I spent a lot of weekends in high school at home watching movies with my parents or going out for ice cream with my mom. While I wouldn't trade the relationships that I have with my parents for anything, I also longed for close friendships with people my age. In my patriarchal blessing I was promised that I would come to find these friendships that my heart so desired and my mission companions were absolutely a fulfillment of that blessing.

    I can vividly remember the day that Sister Fox and I met. It was her first day as a missionary and I was assigned to be her trainer. I had only been serving for three months so we were really figuring things out together! We were assigned to serve in the northernmost area of our mission, Kendallville, Indiana, about two and a half hours away from where our transfer meeting was. At the end of the meeting one of the senior couples handed us a set of car keys and an address and sent us on our way. We plugged the address into our GPS, started driving through the cornfields of the Midwest, and hoped that we were heading to the right place! There wasn't a quiet or dull moment on that car ride. We shared our life stories, and a lot of laughs, and had an instant connection.

I knew that day that Sister Fox would be my best friend for the rest of my life and I was so grateful that I served my mission, even just to find my best friend. We served together in Indiana for three months before Sister Fox was transferred. That was a very hard day for both of us. But, three short months later, we had an unexpected surprise that I'll share from my journal:

April 1, 2014

"Now, I'm sure you're dying to know about the transfer meeting. One of the first missionaries I saw when I got there was Sister Fox's zone leader so I asked if she was coming. He said yes AND she is being transferred and made a Sister Training Leader. My heart skipped at least 3 beats and I told him she was going to be my companion (I was also an STL at the time). He laughed. I commenced to search the building for Sister Fox but she was nowhere to be found, so I took my seat in the chapel. I had my eye on the door until she walked in and I stared at her until we made eye contact. We both freaked out a little and I tried to mouth, "We are going to be companions!!"

As I sat through the transfer meeting, I almost couldn't bear the butterflies in my stomach. I was trying SO hard to push the thought out of my mind that we could be companions because I knew I was setting myself up for devastation when we weren't. President Porter kept catching my eye, though, and I swear he had a mischievous grin. Finally, they started announcing the new companionships. I think I almost had a heart attack.

"In Eastgate 3 Sister Rolfe will be training a new Sister Training Leader in............. SISTER FOX"

The crowd went wild! Seriously. The next few minutes are honestly a bit of a blur, but I know I pushed a few poor sisters out of my way to get to Foxy. I think I almost broke her back when we hugged. We finally stopped hugging and I turned to President Porter and said, "I love you so much!" Sister Porter was laughing so hard at us. By this point, I had embarrassed Sister Fox pretty bad so we took our seats. I couldn't tell you another word that was said the rest of the meeting. I just kept looking at Sister Fox to make sure she didn't vanish or turn into another sister. I was also holding my breath praying President wouldn't get up and say "April Fools!!" Because, yes, of course, transfers were on April Fools Day! But, he didn't! We're still together and it's been the best/craziest week!!

Every missionary we saw that day and the next day at Mission Leadership Council had a miniature reaction of ours. One told us, "I witnessed a miracle today!" I also can't tell you how many times I've been asked in the past week if Sister Fox was my sister—even more than in Kendallville, I think. One of our investigators even asked Sister Fox, "Did you just stare at Sister Rolfe while she was training you so that you could get down all of her mannerisms?? Now we have a blond Sister Rolfe and a brunette Sister Rolfe!" Haha. It is SO good to be back together!!

Hopefully this fun journal entry gave you a little glimpse into the friendship that Sister Fox and I so quickly developed. People from our mission often get us confused and it seems that a lot of them just think of us as the same person! Our mission president actually told us that he would have never put us back together as companions if God hadn't told him to because we got along too easily and that, because of that, God must love us very much! I knew that God was fulfilling His promise to me from my patriarchal blessing and I'm so grateful for that.

However, I think it's also important to share that, as President Porter pointed out, you're not always going to get along with your companions perfectly from the beginning. Most companionships take a little more work than that. When Sister Fox was transferred out of Kendallville I was assigned to train Sister Lawrence. She was a brand new missionary and I was feeling the pressure of being her trainer and setting the stage for the rest of her mission. I worked hard to be an exactly obedient missionary. I was in bed at 10:30 (our assigned bedtime) every night and felt guilty if my prayers kept me on my knees a little past that. I felt strongly that I was supposed to be an example of obedience to other missionaries and I share this example to show you that sometimes I may have taken my call to be exactly obedient a little too far. Sister Lawrence had a more relaxed take on some of the mission rules and with my exactly obedient mindset I just couldn't handle that. I would seriously stress if we weren't following every mission rule perfectly and I felt like I was setting her up for failure if I didn't teach her how to be exactly obedient. This was really putting a strain on our relationship.

I remember one morning when we were supposed to be weekly planning—something you do once a week with your companion to plan and prepare for your upcoming week. Our mission president had given us specific guidelines on how he wanted us to do this planning and that morning it was not going well for us. I would run an idea by Sister Lawrence and she would tell me she didn't care or know the area well enough. I trudged forward and continued to push her to help me. Weekly planning usually takes an entire morning and afternoon to complete and I was getting pretty frustrated about having to do the whole task by myself. Eventually Sister Lawrence started writing letters, something we were only supposed to do on P Days, and completely ignoring me. I am not a confrontational person, but I was seriously about to lose my cool. Before I could explode, though, Sister Lawrence started crying and ran to the bathroom where she locked herself in and still wouldn't speak to me. At this point I couldn't hold in my emotions any longer and I started crying, too. Unfortunately, this wasn't the only time that Sister Lawrence and I both ended up in tears. We were both frustrated with ourselves and each other and couldn't figure out how to work together.

A couple weeks later we went on exchanges with our sister training leaders—the sister missionaries assigned to mentor us. I opened up to my STL and told her that I felt like I was failing as a trainer and that Sister Lawrence and I weren't connecting because of our differing views of obedience. She wasn't sure what we should do so we called our zone leaders. After explaining the situation, one of them asked me what Sister Lawrence's hobbies are—what did she do before her mission? What is her family like? What's her favorite kind of music? I couldn't answer any of his questions. I was so embarrassed. That moment was a big wake up call for me. I was so focused on making Sister Lawrence into the perfect missionary and correcting all of her mistakes that I hadn't even taken the time to get to know her. Although the Savior's name was on my chest, I wasn't representing him very well because that is definitely not how he would have treated his companion. I prayed for his help and began getting to know Sister Lawrence. A saying from our mission president started popping into my mind often: "They won't care how much you know until they know how much you care." He was talking about our investigators but I knew the same applied to my companions. I started asking Sister Lawrence questions about herself and her family. I learned what her interests were and discovered that we even had some of the same hobbies. I began to love her because I began to really know her. We started laughing—a lot. I have a whole page in my mission journal dedicated to our inside jokes. We also started teaching a lot. It's much easier to have the Spirit with you when you're focused on loving your companion rather than changing them. Sister Lawrence and I shared some incredible spiritual experiences and actually ended up having three baptisms that transfer in an area that hadn't had any baptisms in months. Some of my favorite memories from my mission are from the transfer we spent together and I can honestly say that I was heartbroken the day that I was transferred out of that area.

President Porter taught that our companions should know what it's like to be in a companionship with the Savior and while I still had a lot to learn, I definitely learned the importance of that statement during my companionship with Sister Lawrence. Rather than praying for God to bless you to have patience with your companions, pray that they'll have patience with you while *you* strive to change and become more like the Savior. During a conversation that I recently had with Sister Lawrence she told me that the more I pushed her at the beginning of our companionship the more she pulled away. We both recognize and are grateful for the changes that we were able to make during our companionship as we learned to focus on changing ourselves and loving one another. She also mentioned that she did end up becoming an exactly obedient missionary—it just took a little love, not coercion, to help get her there. I can't imagine not having the friendship that I now have with Sister Lawrence and I'm grateful that she was patient with me while I learned and grew as a missionary and as a companion. Though all of your companions might not be your best friends, at least not at the start, you can grow to love them as you strive to see them as Christ does.

<u>Ideas for serving/loving your companion:</u>
o Find what's right!
o Pray for them out loud by name
o Pray for them when they're talking to investigators
o Leave them sticky notes with reasons why you're grateful for them or anything that will make them smile
o Make their bed
o Really get to know them and their background and interests. Ask about their family members by name.
o Spend time doing something fun together on P Day
o Tell them why you love them every night before you go to bed (as cheesy as it may sound it will make all the difference in the world)

Not knowing the Gospel well enough

The biggest concern that I had, and that nearly every sister I talked to has expressed as well, was not knowing the Gospel well enough. Let me just start by saying this: you're never going to have all of the answers and that's okay. You are enough. God has called YOU to this work. Yes, you. And yes, He knows that you're imperfect. If He wanted His missionaries to be gospel scholars he wouldn't be sending out teenagers. If you accept His call to serve,

He will expand your capacity to learn in unimaginable ways. Please do not let your fear of not knowing enough hold you back from serving. All that is required of you right now is faith—even faith the size of a mustard seed. And if you're reading this book chances are pretty good that you have that.

I had never read the Book of Mormon all the way through before I received my mission call. Honestly, I didn't begin to really study the scriptures on my own until I had a mission call! I made it a goal to finish the Book of Mormon before I left on my mission and my love for the Gospel and desire to serve grew infinitely as I did just that. I had never read any of the Bible on my own and I felt like there was so much of the Gospel that I didn't know or really understand. Honestly, that terrified me. I remember stressing so many nights while lying in bed because I only knew one scripture mastery by heart; and I was pretty sure it was required of missionaries to know every scripture mastery and more! Guess what my assigned farewell talk topic was? That very scripture. The ONLY one I knew by heart. Helaman 5:12 if you're curious. God knew that this was a concern of mine and when I received that talk assignment I knew that He was telling me that what I knew was enough. It turns out that missionaries aren't actually required to have all of the scripture mastery scriptures memorized and, ironically, scripture mastery isn't even taught anymore.

God wants you as you are, but rest assured He won't leave you as you are. As you devote your whole heart, might, mind, and strength to serving the Lord, He will help you to learn the Gospel deeply and quickly. You will literally be a sponge. It will be an incredible time of your life unlike any other where you will be blessed to spend hours of your day studying the Gospel and the rest of your day sharing it. As you seek to follow the Spirit, you will be given the words to say in the very moment that you need them, as promised in D&C 100:6. The Lord has promised that if you open your mouth, it will be filled (D&C 33:8) and He will not withhold that promise from you when you're seeking to bring His children to Him. In nearly every lesson that I taught as a missionary I had scriptures come into my mind that I didn't even know I knew and, without fail, they were just what that person needed to hear. Be humble and submissive to the Spirit, seek to learn all that you can, and love those that you teach. God will take care of the rest. This is His work. He is cheering for you and supporting you every step of the way. He wants you to be successful! Remember these things when you have doubts and fears creep in because faith and fear cannot coexist.

I'll share just a couple experiences with you where the Spirit took over when my companions and I were willing to listen. As I've read back through these experiences, my heart is so full. It was so hard to choose just a few to share, but I can't wait for you to have so many of these experiences of your own on your mission. You will cherish them forever!

November 24, 2014

"Sister Huber and I have been teaching Greg since the first night we were together (a little before for her). He is one of the most sincere people I've ever taught and we both have grown to care about him very much. As we've taught him, he's struggled with accepting the Book of Mormon because he's been very devoted to the Bible all of his life, but he has sensed the goodness of the Gospel and has sincerely sought answers. 2 Saturdays ago Greg agreed to join us at a baptism! However, he called us a few hours before and informed us he wouldn't be at the baptism or at church the next day. He told us a lot had changed since the night before (when we had an awesome lesson) and he realized he just couldn't accept the Book of Mormon. We were heart broken. He is so sweet and felt so bad and told us that we could come over one last time to talk.

As you can imagine, we prayed our little hearts out to know what to share with him. It was put on both of our hearts to talk to Greg about fasting. Interesting.... The inspiration was pretty clear though, so we decided that is what we would do. Just before we went into Greg's appointment, I had the thought to bring my hymn book. When we got there I asked if we could start with a hymn, something we had never done with him before. I flipped through and stopped at Nearer My God to Thee. As we sang, Greg's eyes filled with tears. The Spirit was so strong. We proceeded to talk to him about fasting and acted like he had never said anything about not meeting anymore. He readily agreed to fast for an answer! He texted us the next day and told us he studied fasting and prayer on lds.org and felt prepared for his fast. We all fasted together the next day. The following evening we visited Greg and he shared his fasting experience with us and informed us that he received the clear answer that he needs to be baptized in December! He said that everything changed when we sang the hymn. That was one of the few times in his life he can remember feeling the Spirit so strongly and the hymn we chose happened to be one of his favorites from childhood. He concluded after the hymn that nothing that made him feel so good could be from the devil, so it must be from God. This led him to have an open heart during his fast. Wow. Greg went from dropping us on Friday to telling us he wants to be baptized on Saturday."

October 27, 2014

"My testimony of the Gospel has been strengthened so much this week and it all started on Monday when we went to the Creation Museum (a Christian museum about the book of Genesis-- the Creation of the world). One of our investigators works there and offered to get us free passes. We had heard a lot about it and were really excited! When we got there, he and his wife met us up front and told us one of the directors wanted to meet us and show us around. Wow, awesome! We met up with him and he was really nice and told us he wanted to explain what the museum was all about before we started. So, he starts in on his spiel and oh boy we had no idea what we were in for. He basically attacked us and everything we believe in. He kept saying things like, "*some people* believe *this* and that is just nonsense," "you don't believe **everything** Mormons believe do you?" "*This teaching* **clearly** goes against the Bible and would be ridiculous to believe."

We tried to remain cordial and non-confrontational. I was silently praying the whole time that I would know what to do and what to say and that I would be able to be kind and confident about my beliefs. He kept trying to trick us into saying certain things or trap us with our words, but with the help of Heavenly Father we were given exactly the right words to say. Finally, after an hour of this he ended by basically telling us we would be damned because we don't believe in the "right" Jesus. It was terrible. I kept thinking about Elder Holland and his talk about being backed up to the wall of your faith and how when you are being attacked you are standing shoulder to shoulder with the best life this world has ever seen, Jesus Christ. I know that although this hour was one of the most difficult I've yet experienced, I was no doubt standing shoulder to shoulder with my Savior. I felt his name on my badge in a very real way and knew that I was representing Him. I was able to share my testimony in a bold yet loving way and felt very good about how Sister Bowers and I were able to handle the situation because it definitely was not us, it was Heavenly Father. If we had been left alone in that moment we probably would have been in tears and left without the right words, but God will not and did not desert us."

August 12, 2013

"Next is Dave. He's a recent convert and is really struggling. He's in and out of the hospital all the time and went in, again, this week. Sis. Parker and I felt very strongly we needed to go see him Thursday but we had district meeting. While we were getting ready we both had the prompting again so we dropped our blow dryers and called him. Turns out he was out of our area! Ah, but we were prompted!! So, we called the zone leaders and got permission and were off to downtown Cincy! Miracle of all miracles we didn't get lost. So we get to the hospital and realize we only have about 20 minutes and we have no idea what to say but it better be powerful because we've used a ton of our miles and we're way outside our area! When we walk into his room, he's surrounded by doctors and social workers and things are a little crazy. Finally we sit down with him and still have no idea what to say. So we read a scripture and suddenly it hits both of us: Dave and his wife need to go to the temple to be sealed. We ask him what he thinks and he tells us there's no way he wants to be with her forever. (seriously?) So we keep talking. And we are filled with the spirit. And we are BOLD. And the words are not ours. And for the first time since knowing him I'm able to have a serious conversation with Dave (he's the biggest tease/jokester/sarcastic person I've met). And the things we say actually hit him and he tells us to pour his coffee down the sink. After I said the closing prayer, Dave was in tears and told us we had no idea what this meant to him. He asked when we were both going home and told us we would go to the temple with him and his wife before then. Wow! wow wow wow. If you only knew Dave you would know this is a miracle!! We were in awe. Our Father in Heaven knows our needs. I am so grateful every day to be a tool in his hands. My testimony grows every time I open my mouth because it is never my own words that come out.

July 14, 2014

"Had the craziest/ best missionary night of my life. Tuesday, Foxy and I spent our last 3 hours of the day at the church because we had friends coming to the family history center--woo! We ended up filling up the fhc and not having enough room for everyone!!! The hastening is happening :) Anyway, we ended up getting there early with Angela so we were able to give her a chapel tour beforehand and she committed to pray about baptism. Then she went and had an AWESOME experience doing family history. Then Al showed up, but there wasn't room for her so she was really upset. We took her into the chapel to talk and found out her life was basically falling apart. We sang hymns to her and the spirit was so strong. One of her friendshippers came in and literally read my mind by asking Al if she wanted a blessing. She accepted and had one of the most powerful spiritual experiences of her life. She is a very skeptical person, but after the blessing she looked at Bro. P and said, "I have to ask you something. How did you know that I was thinking about not wanting to be alone? Exactly when I thought that, you blessed me that I wouldn't be alone!" He was able to explain to her that he wasn't giving the blessing, Heavenly Father was. Powerful!!! "

I realize that not all of you will have the same concerns that I did, but I hope reading through my experiences has helped you to recognize that no matter what your concerns may be, God will prepare a way for you to accomplish the plans that He has for you. Whether you're concerned about money, school, relationships, or absolutely anything else, I know that God will light your way as you continue to move forward in faith. Just today I had the opportunity to talk with a sister preparing to serve. She was concerned about how she would pay for her mission because her family is not able to support her. We felt the spirit as we talked about different options that might be available to her and moving forward with faith in God. Later tonight, she texted me and let me know that two people had reached out to her this evening and offered to help finance her mission. God is opening doors for this sweet sister because she is acting on the answer He gave her. Answers don't always come as quickly as they did for her today, but with faith on your side, answers will come. God will not leave you comfortless as you dedicate yourself to serving Him.

What I learned in Cincinnati

- Open your mouth
- Truly listen to people when they talk rather than thinking about the next thing you will say. Trust that the Spirit will provide.
- Use your study time wisely! Study with specific people and their needs in mind.
- Remember that fear and faith can't coexist
- Remember that you are ENOUGH

YOU'VE GOT THIS, SISTER

Sister Parker and I after my first transfer meeting

Sister Fox and I in our apartment in the Blackham's basement

With Mama B and Papa B the night before I left Eastgate for the second time

Sister Ryan and I outside the Louisville, KY Temple

REXBURG, ID

February 2019

Before I knew it, I was on an airplane back to Utah and my mission had come to an end. What a bittersweet experience that was. There is so much I could say about coming home, but I will save that for another book. To wrap this up, I want to tell you about what my life looks like right now. I'm sealed to my very best friend who I love with all of my heart. We have the sassiest, sweetest little girl and the happiest, most laid back baby boy. I am blessed to spend every single day playing and learning with my two babies. My husband, Ben, and I own an online business and he gets to work from home. So, like I mentioned before, we basically are living out my dream of being together all the time. My best friend, Sister Fox as you know her, comes over with her son almost every day for play dates. Our kids are best friends, too, and we're convinced that they're going to get married someday. We live down the street from a beautiful temple. We're doing our best to work our way through the Come Follow Me booklet as a family each night. And, most importantly, despite our struggles and weaknesses, we have the Spirit in our home.

Because of my mission, I am the wife and mother that I am. I am not perfect. Not even close. But I am living the life that I've dreamed of and prayed for and my mission played an irreplaceable role in bringing me here. I wouldn't know my husband or best friend if it weren't for my mission. Because of my mission, I have a close and personal relationship with my Savior. Because of my mission, I know and live the Gospel more deeply and personally. Because of my mission, I seek personal revelation every day. One of the greatest blessings that came from my missionary service was how it prepared me to be a wife and mother. Your mission is truly the MTC for the rest of your life, as my MTC president's wife once said. I believe that I was sent to this Earth to have a family and my mission helped me to more deeply understand, and prepare for that. From my mission journal:

"Then, as I sat pondering family (in the temple), everything really connected. All of the articles I had studied about the temple had the common theme of family—we go to the temple to understand our role in our eternal family and to create/strengthen our earthly families. I can't exactly describe how it all fell into place in my mind, but basically I know I am on my mission to prepare for my future family. That is the whole reason I am here on this Earth and I know it without a doubt—I can feel it in my spirit. I am here to have a family and there is no way on this Earth I would have been prepared for that without my mission." (March 2014)

Marriage

I've felt hesitant to share this part of my story because I don't want it to come across the wrong way. But it's part of my story, my favorite part actually, and I can't finish this book without sharing it. So here we go.

When Sister Fox and I were serving in Kendallville we relied a lot on encouragement from our zone leaders and other missionaries in our area. We were both brand new missionaries in a new area that hadn't had sisters for over 20 years. There was a lot of pressure on us and we needed all the cheerleading that we could get. Our zone leaders were, luckily, great cheerleaders and would check in on us often to hear about miracles we were seeing and encourage us to keep moving forward and rely on the Lord. They really helped shape Sister Fox and I into the missionaries and leaders that we would be throughout the rest of our missions. I was always so impressed by their cheerfulness and willingness to do whatever the Lord asked of them. They really made our zone feel united as a family. We were on fire and the rest of the mission was noticing. It was a miraculous time in my mission that I'll never forget. One of our Zone Leaders, Elder Martin, ended up serving around me throughout the rest of his mission. We became good friends and I learned a lot from him about what it means to devote your whole self to the work. I honestly didn't know how he did it. I'm pretty sure you can ask any person who came in contact with him throughout his mission and they'll tell you that he was a good friend who made them feel important. When Elder Martin went home I sent him an email thanking him for his example and telling him how he had affected me and those who had served with and around me. And he didn't respond!

Fast forward three months and it was my time to come home. I quickly became Facebook friends with most of the missionaries I had served around, including Elder Martin. We chatted about the mission and what we were both up to and I just so happened to be moving to Provo for school that weekend (he was living in Salt Lake) so we decided to get together. We met up at Temple Square the Sunday after I got home and spent four hours walking and talking. It was hands down one of the best, happiest nights of my life. He, now Ben (which was really hard to get used to), just had that happiness about him that I couldn't seem to stay away from. The next weekend he took a road trip to St. George with me for my homecoming talk and we went to the temple with some of my family. And, as you can guess, the rest is history! We knew that we would return to that temple one day and be sealed. And four short months later that is exactly what we did. God was not kidding when He told me at the end of my mission that it was time for me to go home and start a family. I didn't realize quite how quickly that would come to pass but I wouldn't change anything about our story!

Now, I have to add that I definitely did not serve a mission to find my husband. If that is your mindset while serving, you're going to miss out on a lot of other incredible experiences and you're probably going to miss the whole point of your mission. My heart was locked, and so was Ben's, and because of that we were able to get to know each other on a strictly platonic basis in a very spiritual setting. For us, God needed this to be the basis of our relationship. I think part of the reason for that was because of how quickly things would fall into place and progress for us after our missions. We're still learning all the reasons why. I do want to use this story to point out, though, that Ben and I would not have met if it weren't for both of us following the promptings that we each received to serve a mission. Your husband might be serving in another mission, going to college, or waiting to meet you at your first job after your mission. But wherever he is, you'll be more prepared to meet and marry him after you've faithfully served the Lord, if that's God's plan for you. He will bless your marriage and future children in so many ways. I also want to use this example to point out that if you feel the conviction to serve and choose not to follow it, you may miss out on miracles that God has prepared for you. Whether that be a husband, a lifelong friend, a job opportunity, a change of heart, or anything else the Lord sees fit. He will lead you to the best possible outcomes for your life if you follow the path He sets before you.

Motherhood

A blog post that I wrote as I reflected on my first year of motherhood more fully explains how God really utilized my mission to prepare me to fulfill the rest of my life's mission:

My role as a mother is very precious and sacred to me. A mom is something I've (almost) always wanted to be. I grew up dreaming of having 5 kids and being a great homemaker but it always seemed like just that—a dream. When I graduated high school suddenly it all seemed much more real and forthcoming and I got scared. Everyone teased me about going off to BYU and getting married my first semester of college and even though I was actually really excited to get married I wasn't ready yet. I graduated high school with BIG dreams. I wanted to get an education and I wanted to do that through traveling and seeing and experiencing the world. I was not about to get married and settle down at 18. But I honestly didn't know if it was okay to have these dreams and ambitions. I loved the Gospel and I had always been taught that it was my calling here on this Earth to become a wife and mother. So was I wrong not to want that right away? I remember walking with my mom one morning and asking her if it was bad that I felt this way. I told her that I did want to be a mom—someday—but I didn't have that desire just yet. She comforted me and told me that was perfectly fine. She assured me that when the time was right I would feel it and know it. She probably doesn't even remember that conversation and has no idea how much comfort those simple words brought me.

Well, my dreams came true. After successfully finishing a semester at BYU unwed I moved to London to study abroad. After that I headed on my next adventure—serving a mission. While serving as a full time missionary I grew to love and appreciate mothers. I spent a lot of time with young moms in the wards and branches I served in and I couldn't help but admire them. And—

finally—I wanted to be just like them. Throughout my mission my desire to be a mom grew and grew. I no longer *believed* that my purpose in life was to be a mother—I **knew** it. I knew it was true for me personally. I had sacred experiences with my Heavenly Father where He taught me just how sweet and precious a calling motherhood truly is. I have so much love and respect for mothers and I KNOW He does, too. I could go on and on about the sacredness of motherhood. Near the end of my mission I received a very clear impression from God that it was time for me to go home, get married, and start a family. I didn't have anyone waiting for me so I had no idea how this was going to happen but I trusted in Him and told Him I would follow His plan.

Four short days after getting home from my mission I walked around temple square with Ben. Shortly after that we were talking about marriage and shortly after that we were talking about having a family. Nine quick months after our first date I was pregnant with our first baby girl. My journey through motherhood since then has been the hardest, most sacred and rewarding thing I've ever done. I truly believe that it is my divine calling here on this Earth to be a mother, a co-creator with God, to bring His precious spirits into this world. And he prepared me for that, in a million different ways, through my missionary service.

KAYLA ROLFE MARTIN

Ben and I on our wedding day

Our most recent family picture (October 2019)

MOVING FORWARD

What are your goals and dreams? What is your vision for your life? Deep in your heart, what do you believe God wants you to become and achieve?

How will serving a mission help you to become that?

If you're feeling the Spirit right now, God is trying to tell you something and I hope that you'll listen. And that you'll take a minute to write down whatever thoughts are coming into your mind. Revelation recorded is revelation available in times of need. The next step is the hardest and it's going to take a little faith. I invite you to act on those thoughts, feelings, and impressions that you're having. I know they will shape your life in ways only God can. I'm sure I didn't speak to all your questions and concerns about serving a mission, but I hope the Spirit touched your heart as you read. God has called all of us to His work and that looks a little different for each of us. The ways in which He speaks to you and the plans that He has for your life are unique. As you courageously act on the promptings He gives you, you'll be able to fulfill each calling that He has for you and you'll feel the Spirit's guidance as you do. I plead with you to ignore the urge to compare yourself and your journey to those around you. God knows what is best for you and can see the bigger picture when you cannot.

One of my callings was to serve a mission and I believe that God has also called upon me to share my experiences in this book. To say I feel inadequate to be the one writing this and putting it out there for you sisters to read is probably an understatement, but as I've put my own doubts aside and have done my best to follow

God's plan I've been able to witness the Spirit working through me in order to make this into the book that you need. God has continually reminded me of an experience that I had with my mission president's wife after a zone conference on my mission. She and I were sitting in the chapel talking about the missionary age change and how incredible it was to have so many sisters serving in our mission and in missions all around the world. She told me that God needs sister missionaries—that we are changing lives and that He is changing our lives through our service. We're being prepared to be the mothers that He needs for the next generation. She then went on to tell me that the excitement of the age change will wear off and that it will be up to me to go home and share my experiences with as many sisters as I can. I felt the Spirit so strongly when she told me that and I knew that not only was Sister Porter calling on me to share my experiences, but that God was as well. I had no idea how exactly I would do that, but when the prompting to write this book came into my mind I immediately felt the Spirit testify to my heart that this was part of God's plan. I've done my best to be an instrument in His hands and to convey through these words what He needs you to hear.

In the words of our beloved prophet, President Russell M. Nelson, "My dear sisters, we need you! We need your strength, your conversion, your conviction, your ability to lead, your wisdom, and your voices. We simply cannot gather Israel without you. I love you and thank you and now bless you with the ability to leave the world behind as you assist in this crucial and urgent work. Together we can do all that our Heavenly Father needs us to do to prepare the world for the Second Coming of His Beloved Son."

He knows of your incredible potential and I hope that you've had a glimpse of it as well. I hope that you have felt the Spirit testifying to you that YOU. ARE. ENOUGH.

You've got this, sister.

Bibliography

Holland, J. R. (1999). Cast Not Therefore Away Thy Confidence. Retrieved from https://speeches.byu.edu/talks/jeffrey-r-holland_cast-not-away-therefore-your-confidence/

Holland, J. R. (2000). Missionary Work and the Atonement. Retrieved from https://www.lds.org/study/ensign/2001/03/missionary-work-and-the-atonement?lang=eng

Nelson, R. M. (2018). Becoming Exemplary Latter Day Saints. Retrieved from https://www.lds.org/general-conference/2018/10/becoming-exemplary-latter-day-saints?lang=eng

Nelson, R. M. (2018). Sisters' Participation in the Gathering of Israel. Retrieved from https://www.lds.org/general-conference/2018/10/sisters-participation-in-the-gathering-of-israel?lang=eng

Note: To connect with me, and other sisters preparing to serve, follow my Facebook and Instagram pages:

Facebook: You've Got This Sister

Instagram: @youvegotthissister

Contact me at youvegotthissister@gmail.com

To read more of my mission experiences, visit my missionary blog:

sisterkaylarolfe.blogspot.com

Made in the USA
Middletown, DE
29 March 2024